KENT VERSES

Edited By Sarah Olivo

First published in Great Britain in 2018 by:

Young Writers
Remus House
Coltsfoot Drive
Peterborough
PE2 9BF
Telephone: 01733 890066
Website: www.youngwriters.co.uk

FOREWORD

Young Writers was created in 1991 with the express purpose of promoting and encouraging creative writing. Each competition we create is tailored to the relevant age group, hopefully giving each child the inspiration and incentive to create their own piece of writing, whether it's a poem or a short story. We truly believe that seeing it in print gives pupils a sense of achievement and pride in their work and themselves.

Our latest competition, Monster Poetry, focuses on uncovering the different techniques used in poetry and encouraging pupils to explore new ways to write a poem. Using a mix of imagination, expression and poetic styles, this anthology is an impressive snapshot of the inventive, original and skilful writing of young people today. These poems showcase the creativity and talent of these budding new writers as they learn the skills of writing, and we hope you are as entertained by them as we are.

CONTENTS

Oscar Cosier (10)	51
Phoebe Paterson (10)	52
Lily Holden (10)	53
Kacper Sidor (10)	54
Oliver Joy (10)	55
Calleigh Stock (10)	56
Julia Elzbieta Rachwalik (10)	57

Park Way Primary School, Maidstone

Timeo Brunet Bigot (7)	58
Isla Clarke (6)	59
Cameron Anderson (7)	60
Alicia Maxwell (7)	61

Smarden Primary School, Smarden

India Star Duncanson (10)	62

Snodland CE Primary School, Snodland

Zoe Bussey (10)	64
Sonny Bowman (10)	65

St Paul's CE Primary School, Swanley

Grace Lucie Goddard (9)	66
Mia Hennessy (8)	68

St Paulinus CE Primary School, Crayford

Vanessa Idiagbonya (8)	70
Hannah Odelade (8)	72
Raisa Macfoy (8)	74
Titilope Okuleye (8)	76
Joelle Nhyira Marfo (8)	78
Tabitha Olanrewaju (8)	80
Beth Rogers (8)	82
Temitope Temilolu-Moustapha (8)	84

Reuben Tunstall (7)	86
Anayah Bolawole (8)	88
James Agbaje (7)	90
Luke Pitts (7)	91
Zion Makanjuola (8)	92
George Newman (7)	93
Teni Apata (7)	94
William Berry (7)	95
Finley Martin (8)	96
Isaac Rayner (7)	97
Ben Butler (8)	98
Olivia Makanjuola (8)	99
Ronnie Bruce (8)	100
Bracken Rutter (8)	101
Delina Yosief (8)	102
Emmanuel Sanusi (7)	103

St Simon's RC Primary School, South Ashford

Mollie Moore (8)	104
Lorena Francesca Bulla (8)	106
Zhyanne Sevilla (8)	107
Karolina Grudzien (8)	108
Evie Miller (7)	109
Anna Repinska (8)	110
Madison Moore (8)	111
Dawid Szarafinski (8)	112
Alicia Pawlowska Louis (8)	113

The Academy Of Woodlands, Gillingham

Louise Hobbs (10)	114
Samuel Adewumi-Abogunloko (10)	116
Rhea Gowda (10)	117
Anton Williams (10)	118
Grace Waters (9)	119
Ini Caoimhe Rowaiye (10)	120
Victoria Streater (9)	122
Ashton Boothroyd (9)	124
Lily Dance (10)	125
Kyle Rabey Sumpter (9)	126

Grace Mackenney (10)	127
Taylor-Marie Daws (10)	128
Jaslyn Kaur Parmar (10)	129
Bobbie Robertson-Stanley (10)	130
Josh S Kirby (9)	131
Lexi Lowin (9)	132
Holly Watson (10)	133
Chloe Higgins (9)	134
Jago Herd (10)	135
George Collins (10)	136

Tree Tops Academy, Park Wood

Brady Aaron Chapman (9)	137
Kieran Aaron Byrne (10)	138
Tayla Champion (10)	139
Amon Rai (9)	140
Chelsea Mount (10)	142
Emma-Louise Matthews (10)	143
Maddison Scott (10)	144
Toby-Lee William Prebble (9)	145
William Steel (10)	146
Taohil Islam (9)	147
Dibya Rai (10)	148
Faith Edmonds (10)	149
Kayley Watt (10)	150
Joshua Baldock (9)	151

Wickham Court School, West Wickham

Amelia Joyce Mitchell (10)	152
Vaonaïshe Mtombeni (10)	153

THE POEMS

The Fluffatarianigan

I thought I saw a monster in my bed!
It had five googly eyes,
With fangs so scary,
And talons so long,
With antenna on its head,
Its colour so golden.

I was scared at first,
But I looked again and saw it smiling,
I smiled back and stretched my hand to it,
It came it and I saw it was shy.

I asked what its name was,
And it said, "Fluffy."
"Fluffy?" I said. "But you look too scary for a name like that!
"Where are you from?" I asked.

"I am from a planet called Fluffatarianigan."
"Fluffatarianigan?" I said,
"What a mouthful!"
"Yes, it's a very friendly planet!"

Daniel Ibechukwu (9)
Belvedere Junior School, Belvedere

The Mysterious Mermaid Monster

A long time ago
Far, far away
Only Merry the mysterious mermaid could stop the tide.
Merry the mysterious mermaid was very pretty
On the island which was very sandy
She wasn't sinister and evil
Or blood-red eyed
Merry had bright blue eyes
Which matched the bright blue skies!
But one day, someone nearly spotted her
And she needed to hide.
Her shells were hard as anything
And had to be washed every day
Every day, she loved to go and play
When she flicked her magical tail
She'd turn all dry
Sometimes she'd wish that she could fly.

Shelby Stokes (10)
Belvedere Junior School, Belvedere

The Fire Monster

Sizzling, simmering, boiling, bubbling water,
the fire monster wakes,
watch the fire monster wake.

Deep in the chambers, roasting and roasting,
if you dare look into the flaming eyes,
you'll burn more and more.

For no one he seeks does escape,
if he finds them, he'll let the flaming rage
of anger come,
it'll hurt and never heal,
his flaming anger is worth a great deal.

When you're all asleep,
he will come every night,
even in your dreams,
just be ready for flaming rage.

Christine Goodwright (10)
Belvedere Junior School, Belvedere

Jealous Of A King

Mr Billy with eyes of brown,
Mr Billy wants the crown.

He's jealous of the king who cut his parrot's wing,
He wants to be proud when he sees his crowd.

But then a girl comes and says to him,
"Hello, my name is Kim.
"Did you know you're part of the royal family?
"You'll be king next,
"If the king dies early."

I think Mr Billy has learnt his lesson,
Don't you think?
He goes to bed happily,
As his cheeks blush pink...

Prajina Gopikishna (9)
Belvedere Junior School, Belvedere

The Thing Beside Me

My little friend was born on a hill,
he did not steal, neither did he kill.
He looks over the towns, the Earth,
the now grown-up skinny monster
started to know his worth.
One day, he tiptoed to me while I was sleeping,
and when I woke up, I started leaking.
I stuttered and asked for his name,
he screamed and stepped away,
it was pretty lame.
He said sorry and said his name was 'Toothpaste',
I mean, it's not that bad, at least it's not 'Tie Your
Shoelace'!

Maliha Grewal (8)
Belvedere Junior School, Belvedere

My Monster

My monster is hairy, not so scary,
but he might give you a fright!
I'll try to shave off his hair,
so he won't be a scare.
He might have one eye,
but he's still mine!
He came from Mars,
like a star in a hurry.
He is my best friend forever,
we might be different, but that's okay.
His eyes are like stars,
coming back from Mars!
If he goes back to Mars,
my eyes will go dark,
and that's the end of my Monster Poetry!

Zara Alyson Patricia Wilson (8)
Belvedere Junior School, Belvedere

Zoltz

I am a big fluffy monster
People call me Zoltz
If you come too close to me
I'll zap you with five thousand volts

My teeth are sharp
I have one eye
If you come too close
I'll make you die

I'm very mean
I'm very hairy
I'll give you nightmares
I'm very scary
I'm very fast
And I can fly
You won't have time
To say goodbye!

Cameron Cox (8)
Belvedere Junior School, Belvedere

Under The Bed

Did you know?
I have a monster living under my bed.
His name is Wobble,
and he has a very furry head.
He came from Planet Jelly,
with his pet dog, Waffle.

Now, I know you must be thinking,
isn't this awful?
No one can see him,
that isn't very good.
It makes me sad,
and changes my mood.

So I become the monster,
that lives under the bed.

Oliver Smith (8)
Belvedere Junior School, Belvedere

The Leader Of The Shadows

The shadow boy was leader of the shadows,
he was born and raised there.
He was sick of living in the monster world,
and of being a monster,
so he snuck away.
I met him when it was nice and sunny,
forever on that sunny day, we were together,
we were the perfect pair and matched each other.
I said goodbye when the sun went down,
and he stayed hidden forever.

Summer Lloyd (9)
Belvedere Junior School, Belvedere

Monster, Monster

Monster, monster, can't you see?
You can't judge me, 'cause I'm seventeen!

Monster, monster, wherever you are,
I can't see you, so tell me how you are.

Molly, Molly, that's your name,
Don't you want to play my game?

Monster, monster, are you in school?
All I think is *cool, cool, cool!*

Leja Bartusevik (7)
Belvedere Junior School, Belvedere

Candy Monster

C andy is her favourite thing in the world
A mazing colours and features she has
N ever angry, never sad, always up for things
D eadly rotten teeth she has from eating all the candy
Y es, she is kind, yes, she is loving, but her teeth are the worst.

M onsters laugh at her teeth
O h, they are always mean
N ever letting her play with them because of the bad stench.
S ome day, I hope they let her play their games.
T here was only one monster who let her play
E veryone started to copy the nice monster and let her play
"R eunited with the candy monster!" everyone said!

Eva Grace Payne (9)
Bredgar CE Primary School, Bredgar

Spark

S he smiles every day and never gives up,
P lays with her friends and goes to theme parks,
A n intelligent young monster with lots of good
    ideas,
R ides her bike,
K nows how to be crazy.

Matilda Christie (9)

Bredgar CE Primary School, Bredgar

Disastrous Dean

Disastrous Dean is yellow, pink and green.
He is big, clever and strong
And has a bit of a pong.
He has three big eyes compared to his size.
He tells the truth and never lies.
Dean lives in a cave that's nice and warm.
He likes to dance and rave till dawn.
He eats lots of food and hates ice cream
But drinks pond water in-between.

Isabelle Ann Stevens (8)
Hollingbourne Primary School, Hollingbourne

Grizzly Gia

Gia's very hairy
And has very big claws
This beast is very scary
And has very big jaws

His grizzly shape
Makes him hard to spot
He hides up in tall buildings
But complains a lot

About being a statue
All day, all week
But when he flies away
You will hear his magnificent shriek

Once, he went on an adventure
Far, far away
He used up the whole week
But it only took a day!

On the grasslands
We found a high tower

Swept into the place
Then grabbed a princess to devour

When he got back home
From his holiday
He was still as a statue
On the Shard he lay

Gia's very hairy
And has very big claws
This beast's very scary
And has very big jaws.

Nayeli Onuaha (8)
Hollingbourne Primary School, Hollingbourne

Fang's Alien Adventure

Fang has one green eye,
She can be a little shy,
With her mermaid tail,
And wings as thin as a veil,
Fang's wings are red,
She has a crack in her head,
Fang lives in the sea,
She made a new friend called Bea,
They went to a castle to see some guns,
They danced with some soldiers, that was fun,
Two of the soldiers had lots of scars,
Through a window, they could see Mars,
The castle was very cold,
As it was very old.

Louise Smith (7)
Kingswood Primary School, Maidstone

Luigi's Remarkable Restaurant

In Luigi's remarkable restaurant
Things happen that you wouldn't believe.
It started in a kitchen many years ago;
Let me take you back and guide you through the show.
Snakes as evil as Sweeney Todd started tearing off his arms.
They squirted poisonous acid into his face
And the Crazy Chef was born.
At first, he looks charming
But stay back, as he's really alarming.
While you're studying the menu
He creeps from the shadows and absorbs you.
Beware if your favourite food is apple pie,
Because that's an awful way to die.
He picks you up and preps you good,
Watch out or you'll become your favourite food.
Mwah, mwah, mwah!

Jake Aherne (11)
Laleham Gap School, Ramsgate

The Adventures Of The Meme And Vine

I met The Meme and Vine Monster in the wet grass forest, he said hi to me.
He was very excited so his teeth turned pretty pink and shiny.
Then he jumped in squelchy mud, splashing his shiny shoes.
He asked me to jump or run, I didn't know what to choose.
Next we found a portal to the Greek Mythology World.
When we went inside, we were spinning around in purple swirls.
We learnt how to build some boats, we also learnt how to fight,
After that, we then got graded, we got them all right!
We then got teleported to the Meme factory,
There were some secret cameras that me and The Meme monster could see.
The man that worked in there was called Memoo,
He was as tall as skyscrapers, even taller than you!

But then suddenly came a horrible tragedy,
The Meme Monster fell inside the Meme machine!
When he came out he was Memes stuck together.
I cried when I found out that he'd be like this
forever.
I went in the magical portal, I also cried.
When I reached home, I shut the front door and
sighed.
I was sad that the Meme Monster was trapped in
his doom,
I walked away with the Memes stuck together
And I keep it as a souvenir in my bedroom.

Jessica Gale (10)
Laleham Gap School, Ramsgate

Omo

Omo,
little and slimy!
His body jiggles like jelly,
even more so when you tickle his belly!

(North forme)
He can be kept as a pet,
make sure he's not caught in a net,
otherwise he'll need a trip to the vet,
and that will make him really upset!

(East forme)
When he sees you, he's quite malicious,
he might find you very delicious!
He can be so unkind,
it will blow your mind!
With an acidic bite,
what a fright!

(West forme)
She is so shy,
she usually won't reply!
She's super fast,
it will make you gasp!
She might be a vegetarian,
but she acts like a barbarian!

(South forme)
She is eco-friendly,
because she eats dung!
They are nearly extinct,
she is quite distinct!

Harvey Jack Weavill (10)
Laleham Gap School, Ramsgate

The Arctic Robin

The Arctic Robin's eyes gaze into your soul,
With talons as black as coal,
It has webbed feet,
The feathers are like a comfy sheet.

The creature is always kind,
Yet, it has a tiny mind,
Its food lives down low in a burrow,
So it lands in the snow.

The robin spots its food,
Now it gets crude,
The food digs a hole,
And that takes its toll.

The robin sticks down its beak,
In search of the food that it does seek,
An unwary ant crawls into its mouth,
It then flies south.

As it descends due to gravity,
The scent of Arctic wind fills its nasal cavity,

Its mouth waters at the thought of food,
So it turns back in hopes of having a feast, that's true.

Mark Nicolas Sidney Taylor (11)

Laleham Gap School, Ramsgate

The Rex

The Rex was born in a swamp,
It had skin and eyes like a map,
It smelt like boogers and had the face of a man,
It was bad and always mad.

It left the swamp on an adventure,
It needed to be kind, but it couldn't,
It had to be bad.
It came on the beach and made people sad,
I trapped the Rex in a hole I made.

The tide came in and the Rex got mad as a tiger,
It said, "I will get you!"
But sizzled and died.
I became the Rex!

Jonathan Vorster (10)
Laleham Gap School, Ramsgate

What Is It?

It's slithery and it's slimy,
It's thick and it's grimy

It's big and it's long,
And it really smells of pong.

Is it real or is it not
Or will it tie you up in knots?

So check your closet at night
Or it will squeeze you really tight.

So stay in bed, don't get out,
He will make you scream and shout.

His name is Worm,
He will make you squirm.

Max Aisawi (11)
Laleham Gap School, Ramsgate

Dave

This creature lives in the forest
Has four legs and isn't Boris
David is his full name
He has no friends to play a game.

He has one eye
To see the sky
He has white fur to keep warm
Protected from the storm.

He uses his big ears to hear
But his teeth are what you should fear
Dave is friendly and kind
He has a beautiful mind.

Dylan James (10)
Laleham Gap School, Ramsgate

Twenty-Four Hours With An Indonesian Fish Bird

The Indonesian Fish Bird,
With tail feathers bright,
Day will soon be turning to night,
Now it is bedtime.

Early in the morning,
It is time to go a-hunting,
Now we do some spying,
Prey is underwater, look out!

Time to dive down,
Here we go... caught it!
Let's head home now,
Time for some colony battles.

Robin Mummery (10)
Laleham Gap School, Ramsgate

Lightning Flash

He comes out when he hears lightning
At the speed of sound
He will pick herbs out of your gardens
Taking them home and leaving chocolate behind
It's hard to see as it's hidden
Sometimes you can see
The diamond-shaped teeth marks
He leaves behind in your herbs.
He also finds cars
Picks the locks
And drives away!

Zane Eley (9)
Laleham Gap School, Ramsgate

Crusher

Crusher the monster was born in a bin
He is very smelly, with teeth that can
chew through tin

He lives on the rubbish people throw away
Nobody can catch him, even on 'empty the bin' day

One day, I was hoping to catch him
I heard a growl when I threw my cake in the bin

Crusher looked up with big scary eyes
I nearly fell over from the shock and surprise
I shouted out, "Crusher, I've got you now!"
Crusher shouted back, "Wow!"

Maybe he realised he made a mistake
Or maybe he was enjoying the chocolate cake

I quickly slammed down and locked the bin lid
The next day, the dustmen came
So they got rid of him.

Christos Adamou Triantopoulos (7)
Marian Vian Primary School, Elmers End

Googly Home

I live in a magical forest with five friendly monsters:
Siv, Piv, Niv, Giv and Tiv...

I am Googly, I have knobbly knees
and great big eyes
the size of four big mince pies.
I live by a lake
where the waters are opaque
and the trees grow sweets
and the mud underneath is a tasty treat.
Bubblegum stands instead of grass
and the gobstoppers last and last.

I look at this place
while my monster friends race
I say, "Come on Giv, keep up the pace!"
Then Tiv comes in second place
while the other two come last and look
deep in disgrace!

I see chocolate bunnies jumping all over the place
and then they come to give you a taste!

You won't forget the taste on your tongue
from the wine gums
that hang low from the sun
and the candyfloss clouds
that tickle your tum.

Candyland is what I'll call it
so do come along and make sure you explore it.
From candy canes to liquorice cuttings
there isn't a thing we don't have for your stomach.

I love this place full of taste
my monster home
the place I own
and will never moan.

This is Candyland, a place I like best
where I can drift off when I need a rest
and dream of this place
with a smile on my face.

Mia Jennifer Schoburgh (8)
Marian Vian Primary School, Elmers End

Monster Mash

Monsters are every shape
slippery and slimy
and live on Planet Bong
making mash-up songs.
They eat your washing
when you're asleep!
They throw your rubbish on the street
and eat the bin, of course.
They have fangs and turn to rats
they turn to every creature.
They take all your candy
and snap their jaws in laughter
and roast everything in sight.
They can have breath
as stinky as can be
and make their lunch
out of a bee.
They take some mud to Planet Bong
and make a mud bath on Planet Bong.
They go and fly in gravity
and eat slime jelly.

They are spotty
and have sticky pads on their paws.
They're scary and happy
all the time.
They have fiery wings to fly
and spaceships to go to different planets
or around the world.
When you see them
you run away in fear.
They play and do everything scary and fun
and have food made out of eyeballs.

Sara Sriupsaite Syed (8)

Marian Vian Primary School, Elmers End

Nelly The Friendly Monster

My secret pet monster
lives in my bedroom.

On the days I have homework
he leaves me alone
but when it's bedtime
I hear him groan.

Nelly the monster
that is his name.
He tidies my room
while I'm playing games.

So very cute
with a fluffy belly
sometimes we sit together
and watch the telly.

There are times Nelly hides
when he hears Mum and Dad.
If they find him
I will be sad.

Every night
I give him a treat
sometimes a sandwich
sometimes a sweet.

Really, Nelly is my good friend
monster and Sophia
friends 'til the end.

Sophia Adamou Triantopoulos (7)
Marian Vian Primary School, Elmers End

Ghost Fluffy

Don't go near Ghost Fluffy, don't go near,
Don't go near Ghost Fluffy, or you will hear...

The rumbling of his tummy,
Rumble, rumble, rumble,
The grumbling of his mummy,
Grumble, grumble, grumble.

Don't go near Ghost Fluffy, don't go near,
Don't go near Ghost Fluffy, or you will hear...

The scratching of his claws,
Scratch, scratch, scratch,
The stroking of his paws,
Stroke, stroke, stroke.

Don't go near Ghost Fluffy, don't you dare,
Ghost Fluffy is Ghost Fluffy,
'Cause Ghost Fluffy isn't there.

Ellie Clifford (8)
Marian Vian Primary School, Elmers End

The Friendly Monster

Molly is a friendly monster,
who lives in Monster Land.
She loves to make big castles,
with shells and golden sand.
One day, she tried to jump on a cloud,
and fell right through!
She landed in a puddle,
of sticky green goo.
When her friends saw her,
they had a good laugh,
then took her home,
for a nice hot bath.
When she was finished,
her friends had gone home,
so she sat outside and looked at the stars,
feeling sad and alone.

Chloe Jessica Petersen (8)
Marian Vian Primary School, Elmers End

The Dragon

The dragon was a fire-breathing type of dragon,
It had long antennae and a long neck.
It had small glowing eyes,
It had giant fangs and a scary face.
It stunk of smoke and ash,
Its long, dirty fangs sticking out of its gums.
The dragon had long scratches all across its body,
It had five red glowing eyes,
It had a mean look and a cunning grin,
The dragon was the meanest thing you could
ever meet.

Elliot Dobson (7)
Marian Vian Primary School, Elmers End

The Monster Under My Bed

A frightful monster hides under my bed,
His gigantic eyes are shining bright red,
Teeth like knives in enormous jaws
Scraping walls with his sharp white claws.
If you see him, he is so hairy,
You might think he is very scary.
People say that he is not there,
Yes he is, so please beware!

Hattie Jones (8)

Marian Vian Primary School, Elmers End

Lurking

M onsters lurking
O n the atmosphere
N ow destroying stuff
S ee scary eyes
T ell your friends
E veryone's scared
R are.

Cynthia Moigboi (7)
Marian Vian Primary School, Elmers End

Google Fangs

Goggle Fangs was born near a volcano,
And this is very important, you know,
Goggle Fangs *cannot* be trusted,
Everyone around the world is digusted.
One day, that fateful day,
A young boy named Ray,
Wandered into a small cave,
"Hello?" he called. "Dave?"
"I'm here," Dave said,
"What's that in red?"
"Hello!" said the beast,
It was happy, at least.
We all shook hands,
Then I saw the fangs,
It smiled and turned,
Then our hearts burned,
My body started to stiffen all over,
When I realised we'd been taken over,
It was already too late,
We were set out on plates,

Now it truly was the end,
For me and my good friend.

Abigal Ellen Watson (11)
Northumberland Heath Primary School, Erith

My Smile, The Monster

I saw a star falling down
When I came home in my favourite gown
It fell into my yard
Right next to my pet guard
My pet started to bark
That's when I realised it was still dark
As dark as if midnight was there
I felt my eyes glare
I saw a glimpse of light
Lightning lighting up
Some blue fire I saw
I thought, *I better see what it is*
Because I heard a hiss
I realised it was my fuzzy friend
He had a little bend
On his antennae
He had a foe called Spot
Who was a little dot
I went to meet him
My blue-furred friend.

Kinga Smyk (10)
Palm Bay Primary School, Cliftonville

My Blobby

He came out of nowhere
Like an overgrown carrot rolling on the floor
He flew up like an ascending angel in the air
Then he slipped and landed near my door.

As puffy as a polar bear
He stood up with aplomb
He waddled over and gave me a scare
He waddled closer to me and my toys.

He picked up one of my toys
Jumping around with a toy car
He was playing on the floor with the car
And jumped up and smiled
All the boys looked at him
Questioning what he was doing
And he kicked a ball over to the boys
And I called him 'Blobby'.

Lewis Joshua Philps (10)
Palm Bay Primary School, Cliftonville

Vivi, My Forever Monster

He came out of nowhere,
Like a bird flying through the air,
He said his name was Vivi,
Like he was extremely fair.

He was as slimy as a slug,
But that didn't bother me,
He grabbed a bottle of water and the noise went,
glug, glug, glug,
I told him my name and we both went to the sea.

He bought a bag of chips,
As his stomach was rumbling,
Then he turned around and tripped,
And went off tumbling.

His skin turned blue,
And he grew to the height of six foot two,
Vivi is my forever monster!

London McSweeney (10)
Palm Bay Primary School, Cliftonville

Destructo

Destructo comes from Planet Benze,
But he has no real friends.
He lands on Earth,
But starts ripping Tim's garden turf!
He blows up the House of Commons,
He is like a bolt of lightning,
Which people think is very frightening!
The Queen is horrified at what she's seen,
And pleads, "Help us! Or is this just a dream?"
Then a boy makes him laugh,
(With a very rude fart!)
But this does Destructo no good,
He laughs and laughs until he becomes hot,
Then he exclaims, "Stop! Stop! Before I go pop...!"

Bradley Glover (10)
Palm Bay Primary School, Cliftonville

The Adventure Of Devil's Mutt

Devil's Mutt was born in The Underworld
He was good as gold
But he had a small problem
He didn't have a friend of his own!
Devil's Mutt ventured across hills, mountains
Even across the Pacific Ocean!
At last, he came to rest in a goliath forest
Where he met a fellow called Furball
Furball did not run away at the sight of him
Devil's Mutt blinked his million eyes
He patted Furball on the head with
his clawed tentacle
The orange fluff agreed to become his friend
And they lived happily every after.

Jack Perrin (10)
Palm Bay Primary School, Cliftonville

A Creature At The Beach

At the bottom of the garden,
in a cute, small house,
lived a creature called Puffy,
who was as small as a mouse.
Puffy was lonely,
so she wanted a friend,
she got her things and saw a fly,
and went down to the beach,
she saw the lifeguard and she waved,
she got out her bucket and spade,
and she said hello.
I have a little monster called Puffy,
and she is very fluffy,
and when she was at the bottom of the garden,
she said, "I am your monster to keep,
until the sun is gone."

Lucy Burring (10)
Palm Bay Primary School, Cliftonville

The Mecky Mayhem!

He came from Mars
Down in a spaceship
He fell in a bar
I saw how he barely made it
He waddled up
To my door
He looked like a pup
But seemed pretty poor
He had an arm of metal
And a foot of steel
He picked a petal
And some orange peel
He flushed them down the toilet
And flew across the room
And had to poo!
Now he's forty
And is still a friend,
Whose name is Mecky.

George Maiden-Tilsen (10)
Palm Bay Primary School, Cliftonville

Monster Mayhem And The Monster Slayer

Eyes as red as fire
Claws as sharp as swords
Teeth as pointy as thorns
Fire as hot as a thousand suns
It is Midnight Cobra.
The slayer, who is as brave as a thousand knights'
swords made out of monster root
the only thing that can kill a monster.
His battle has gone on for years and years
but it is time for a new hero
Emily Hofeson
and Emily will defeat him.

Aibhlinn Harman (9)
Palm Bay Primary School, Cliftonville

Running For Your Life!

I was walking in a dark, gloomy forest
and that's when it attacked.
It crunched through trees
smashed into fences
and tore them apart.
I ran and ran
not turning back
then smashed into a tree.
That's when it attacked me
it bit my leg.
"Ow!" I screamed
but nobody heard me.
"Help!" I called
but nobody ever came...

Oscar Cosier (10)
Palm Bay Primary School, Cliftonville

Pink And Fluffy

Boo Hoo the monster is pink and happy
and a little bit dappy
but only because she is in love.
She loves Hairy
but he is a little scary
and he would not be the type for me!
Boo Hoo is pink and fluffy
and awfully cuddly
and I wish she would come back to me.
I can't sleep without her
I'm awfully tired
but she has found true love without me!

Phoebe Paterson (10)
Palm Bay Primary School, Cliftonville

Dip-Who?

Once I found a toy
and named it McCoy
then suddenly, before my eyes
it became alive.
I kept her a secret
and she agreed to keep it.
She said her name was Dip-Dip.
I said mine was Pip-Pip.
I picked her up
but she said, "Hey, what luck
I can walk, you know!"
"Oh, sorry," I said
and then we went to bed.

Lily Holden (10)
Palm Bay Primary School, Cliftonville

The Big Eye Monster

He thought he was very strong
but he was very wrong.
He was very nice
but he had twice the eyes.
He wanted to climb the hill
but he was very ill.
He grinned and fell into the bin
he only just realised he was very thin.
He found a grape
and wiped his face with the sticky tape.
The date was the eighth of May
he hated that day.

Kacper Sidor (10)
Palm Bay Primary School, Cliftonville

Whiplash's Fantastic Adventure

There once was a monster
his name was Whiplash
he was very playful
and liked to smash.
He explored volcanoes
and found loads of abandoned ships
he was rich from all the treasure he found
and had wreck exploring tips.
Whiplash found a sub
with a man inside, eating out of a tub
then they were buddies, great old buddies.

Oliver Joy (10)
Palm Bay Primary School, Cliftonville

The Cute Little Puny Fuffy Monster

I found a cute monster,
who was fluffy and pluffy,
with her little hands,
and her tiny little tummy,
with one little eye,
and two cute cheeks,
you were my monster to keep.
She sat on my shoulder,
with three little feet,
she had two tentacles,
and two little cheeks,
you were my monster to keep.

Calleigh Stock (10)
Palm Bay Primary School, Cliftonville

The Malteser Friendship

Today, I met a creature,
he said he was a teaser,
he took my Malteser!
I found on the floor.
He ran out the door
and crashed his face on the floor.
I ran to say
was he okay?
His name was Jolly Jay.

Julia Elzbieta Rachwalik (10)
Palm Bay Primary School, Cliftonville

Scary Hugs

One day deep in a haunted volcano,
There lived a furry monster called Louis,
He was born in the volcano,
He had molten, crooked teeth,
He was as evil as a dragon,
He loved scaring little kids,
So off he went to scare a little child,
As he was waiting under his private bridge,
As the little girl skipped on the bridge,
The monster bolted up and screamed a roar!
"Oh! You cute thing, let me cuddle you," said the little girl.
"Argh!" screamed Louis.
He ran as fast as he could to his home
And the mean beast with a lion head
Was never to be found again.

Timeo Brunet Bigot (7)
Park Way Primary School, Maidstone

My Pet Monster

My pet monster is blue and likes to eat stew.
My pet monster's legs are purple and green.
My pet monster likes to be seen.
My pet monster's arms are red and yellow.
My pet monster gives a humongous bellow!
My pet monster smells of the seaside.
My pet monster is too big to hide.
My pet monster likes to play Ludo.
My pet monster *has* to win, though!

Isla Clarke (6)
Park Way Primary School, Maidstone

My Monster

My monster is fluffy and pink
he likes to skate at the rink.
He has crooked teeth and a very bad smell
and he lives in a cave on a very high hill!

He has magnetic powers
and controls the weather too!
He has lots of alien friends
but would like to be your friend too.

Cameron Anderson (7)
Park Way Primary School, Maidstone

Slimey The Monster

Slimey the monster was slimy and green
He lived in a cave so he could not be seen.

He liked to play with toys and games
And read me stories when bedtime came.

He looked so scary with ugly feet
But a nicer monster, you would not meet.

Alicia Maxwell (7)
Park Way Primary School, Maidstone

My New Pet

Today I got a new pet,
she is so cute, no regret,
I saw her, rainbow and in all her glory
at a pet store,
but not where you'd think she'd be -
she was on the pet store owner's head!
I told him and he said,
"Hehehe, what a joke!"
The monster gave his head a gentle poke,
I took the creature off his head.
"Tha-that's not a joke!"
He ran off yelling, "Monster, monster!"
I just gave it a hug.
"Bug! Bug, bug, bug!" it yelled.
It jumped on the floor,
and pounced on something pure,
it held it up for me to see,
it looked like her, but a baby!
The creature handed it to me.
"Flakabanan!" it said, lively.

The big one was now on my head,
it seemed to want to go to bed.
I took it off for me to see,
putting down the little baby.
It licked my nose,
then jumped on my toes.
I picked it back up,
now I knew it could stand,
it took a look at its child in its hands.
I walked down the street,
it moving to the beat.
Now I had my pets.

India Star Duncanson (10)
Smarden Primary School, Smarden

The Purple Monster

I opened my eyes one night
and there, in all his might
stood a purple, furry, silver-spotted monster
he smiled at me
and made a plea
that purple, furry, silver-spotted monster
to go for a run
he said, "It'll be fun!"
So myself and the purple, furry,
silver-spotted monster
went for a run
and it was fun.
Where is the purple, furry, silver-spotted monster?
I must've been dreaming
but I had the feeling
I would see the purple, furry, silver-spotted
monster again.

Zoe Bussey (10)
Snodland CE Primary School, Snodland

Fluff Ball

Fluff Ball was a lonely monster
he really had no friends
he was always trying to make them
by keeping up with trends

he tried out roller skating
but couldn't move around
he tried out trampolining
but couldn't leave the ground

he tried out for the football team
but couldn't hit the ball
he had a go at parkour
but ran into the wall

finally, he gave up
and decided he should be
a solo hobo bird watcher
and stay up in his tree.

Sonny Bowman (10)
Snodland CE Primary School, Snodland

The Light In The Dark

Last night, I had a visit from someone in my house,
Was it a bat? No. Not even a mouse.
I was sleepy and tired, what would I do?
What was there? I had no clue!
I opened my eyes. Was it a scare?
But wherever I looked, there was light everywhere.
It made so much noise, it went *thud!*
It had a big coat of fur, eyes red as blood.
It was not dangerous at this rate,
Its legs and arms were not straight.
It would not hurt me, I guarantee,
At that minute, it liked me.
He said, "Do not worry, nor fear."
Then down his face came a tear.
Suddenly, the monster turned off his light,
Then, as he turned around, he said goodnight.
It was helpful, caring and friendly,
Because at that moment, he smiled at me.
He said, "Do not worry or even fear,
Because the Lightness Monster is now here."

I don't care about the monster who will lurk,
Do not warn me. I'm not scared of the dark.

Grace Lucie Goddard (9)
St Paul's CE Primary School, Swanley

Goofy The Goofster

Meet Goofy
his hair is really poofy
his arm is like a snake
is this how much you can take?
Have you seen his hair?
It looks just like a flare.
Ask him one plus one
he will say it's none.
Feel him, he will be fluffy
look at his roller skates, they're made by Muffy.
His arms are really red
how many spikes has he got on his head?
He is a monster, not a fairy
and his name is not Mary.
He used to live on Pluto
and he walks very slow.
He is twenty years old
and is never cold.
He has a big mouth
and he lives down south.

He wears roller skates that are pink
the wheels and shoes link.
He could be your friend
but now we've come to an end.

Mia Hennessy (8)
St Paul's CE Primary School, Swanley

The Plan

Down in a cave
Where monsters lurk and daze
There was one named Cubzoid who had friends named Glub and Sitt
But Cubzoid was the most legit
They were all planning to escape
But Glub said no!
"Don't worry," said Cubzoid. "It's not too late."

"I have a plan," said Sitt with glee.
"Ooh, what's your plan?" asked Glub.
"We crack the code then climb up that tree!"
"I know the code," said Cubzoid.

The code was cracked as fast as a microwave
Glub was thinking he wanted to stay.
"There's the tree," said Sitt.
"It's a rake!" called Cubzoid. "Do we really need it?"
"It's a tree!" exclaimed Sitt.

So up the tree went Cubzoid, Glub and Sitt
But they didn't know they'd gone right into a pit!

"Your chubby cheeks are squashing me!" yelled
Glub.
As fast as a cheetah, creepers in the pit
Started forming into a big lump.
"Argh, we're going to die!" yelled Cubzoid. "Look, a
snake!
"But I'm sure I know how to escape."

Cut, cut, cut, went Cubzoid's claws
His claws were so sharp, they were sharper than a
dragon's jaws
They were free
And they all smiled with great glee.

Vanessa Idiagbonya (8)
St Paulinus CE Primary School, Crayford

The Half Emotion

There is a monster called Havana
One side of her is hot as lava
If you ever see her
She'll probably be eating a jam tart
That's gone off and smells like fart
She is very angry, her head could pop
Her hair will go all floppy like a mop
Havana's cuddly, cute face is so pink
But the other side of her will disturb you
The cute side of her will melt your heart
In Havana's city, she is very popular
You need to control her if she gets angry.

Once, the cute side of Havana
And the angry side of Havana
Got into a big argument
And the angry side nearly bombed with fire
And the cute side nearly burst with hearts
So they split apart and the whole world stomped
The envious evil side went to take over
the universe
The cute, cuddly and cunning side went to have
dinner with the queen of hearts

When evil Havana took over the world
Good Havana's tea party was messed up
The palace danced about and cartwheeled
Good Havana looked hideous
And the queen was stupendous
From that day on, Havana swapped sides.

Good Havana was angry as could be
Bad Havana was happy as flowers.

Hannah Odelade (8)
St Paulinus CE Primary School, Crayford

Queen Diamond

One stormy night in sudden light
A monster came flying like a minotaur
It was called Queen Diamond
She had a long tongue to catch people
She spread kindness to everyone
Her fangs were almost invisible
Diamond had laser beams
She glided on the breath of wings
She was as brave as a lion
She was as cute as a cupcake
She was as smart as an owl.
Queen Diamond had butterfly wings which were
purple and yellow
Queen Diamond was crazy with sweets, so you
weren't to give her any (unless she was good).

Queen Diamond was a dashing monster
With spectacular grades at school
In the end, she saved the day
She was a hero.

She liked pasta peppers with pepper chilli
She was a scary, special shape-shifter
And a very sneaky sausage
A clever person
She had an antenna.

One day, Queen Diamond got so angry
Five of her diamonds broke into thirteen shards
She tried to find them, but instead she got rubies
She had new powers, woo!

Raisa Macfoy (8)
St Paulinus CE Primary School, Crayford

The Monster

He's as big as a pig
As towering as a cyclops, he looks very scary
But he's friendly.
He's big and hairy
He's big and scary
He's kind, big and funny
But he's very clever
And he has a long tongue!
He's brave and he's the one for you
That's what everyone says
He's very intelligent
But I don't know what it is.

Today, I was going on a plane
And my friend was coming
Some of the food had been stolen
We tried to find who stole the food.
We tried and tried.

Then we found a monster
His name was Monsteranic and he came
from Monstertanic.

I was shocked when I heard him speak
And he asked if he could stay with me.
But he couldn't stay.
I said, "I'll come every day
And come to give you food."
He was smooth, soft, stinky and smelly
But his teeth were sharp.
He was the one who stole the food
Because he hadn't had food for a long time.

Titilope Okuleye (8)
St Paulinus CE Primary School, Crayford

The Munching Monster

One day when I was in my room
There was a mysterious noise
I didn't know what it was
But it was something or someone
It came out and it was a, a...
Monster!

The monster was so small
You could win it as a prize in the theatre
She hopped onto my bed
And was shivering in my arms
Like a scared, shivering, small ball of mint.

We started playing games
And the monster was really fast
I decided to name her Mintie
Because she was just like a mint
Soon, my mum came
And I hid Mintie in my cupboard
And carried on with my homework.

At dinner, I told my mum and dad
But they never believed me

My brother winked at me and I winked back at him
After dinner, I showed him Mintie
And he was not frightened at all
We made Monster Slime
But Mintie didn't know how to slide.

I was happy my brother believed me.

Joelle Nhyira Marfo (8)
St Paulinus CE Primary School, Crayford

Blue Flash And Her Special Friends

I have best friends
Big friendship never ends
The streets are rotten
But everyone's forgotten.

When people hear a roar
They come out and have to see
Some monsters say she always raps
Anyway, her eyes go *zap, zap, zap!*

My monster is as creepy as a vampire
She is as fast as a cheetah
She can always seem scary
But only when she sees stuff that's hairy.

She has powers to make werewolves
Only to scare wolves
Her friend, Fireball, has balls of fire
She sometimes uses them to fight in wars.

She is so rude that she can pop your head off
Monsters munch on many mice
We saw the big, chunky cheese moon
Anyway, the monsters went to the moon.

They said they would come back soon
Like bats bouncing boingy balls
But really, now, the streets are raw
And now people are poor.

Tabitha Olanrewaju (8)
St Paulinus CE Primary School, Crayford

A Little Ball Of Fire

A little ball of fire was made one day
Jumped out of a volcano and nothing
got in its way
People screamed, people cried
All FireBall said was, "You're mine!"
She's as small as a football
But as fierce as a lion
FireBall is truly fierce, frightening and fun (in her
own way).

One night, Fireball gathered up her many
monstrous mates
Cool Flash, as fast as lightning
Green Flash, as strong as steel
And Blue Flash, as clear as ice
They made a plan to take over the world.
"Who can we fool?" asked Blue Flash.
"Don't you worry about that!" replied FireBall...

The next day, FireBall and her gang took
over a school
They tricked the children and no one knew

Now, let's try to make this long story short:
They got caught
But escaped and took over the world!

Beth Rogers (8)
St Paulinus CE Primary School, Crayford

An Unlikely Friend

I can hear something downstairs.
What is it, hiding behind the chair?
Scared, frightened, I feel fear.
A shadow, a person? It is not clear.

Imagine midnight eyes.
As dark as the night sky.
Spears creeping from its jaw.
The thought makes me stand in fright, horror and
awe.

Should I check behind the chair, would I dare?
Is that wings, a tail and hair?
Sitting there hiding, trying not to be seen.
It seems shy, scared of me, not mean.

It comes into the light.
Butterfly wings, I think it might take flight.
It moves so fast, so great.
I call and scream, "Wait!"

It stops and turns towards me.
I realise it is not a monster, now I finally see.

I hold out my hand and it takes mine in the end.
It seems I have made an unlikely friend.

Temitope Temilolu-Moustapha (8)
St Paulinus CE Primary School, Crayford

The Doom Boy

Once, there was a bad monster,
Who went to Earth,
He ate many and he had black and grey skin.
His name was Doom Boy,
And he always liked exploding and going *boom!*

He was as fast as a cheetah,
He had gloomy eyes and his terrible face wanted
to attack Earth.

His life was terrible,
And then he went to Earth.
He got to the planet,
And he made people panic.
He took their food,
He was in a big mood.
He was really rude.

He ran, but then he saw someone,
He went to him,
His name was Tim,
The person stopped him,
And then made him be good.

And he gave people back their food,
And then the terrible monster turned into a good monster,
And he went back to Mars.

But one day, he could turn his back on Tim...

Reuben Tunstall (7)
St Paulinus CE Primary School, Crayford

If You See A Monster, It's Okay

If you see a monster
Act as fierce as a lion
And make the other monsters bow down
But oh no, not with this ghoul
She is kind and is a star
She only wants to see her BFF Howleen Wolf
once more
So she packs her favourite, fabulous fashions
And leaves to the open world where she
should not go.
"Howleen!" she cries
But no one comes
What if she left her friend for fame?
But then she sees a tower of pink hair dancing
It is Howleen!
The two girls laugh and hug and ask in unison
"Where have you been?"
So, for this ghostly ghoul, be as cute as a cupcake
Because she doesn't bite.

For some monsters act like them
And learn their ways
And sometimes it's okay
To be afriad.

Anayah Bolawole (8)
St Paulinus CE Primary School, Crayford

The Green Flash And His Friends

A little baby was made one day on Monster Island.
No one got in the way.
He kept munching moths so he could be faster,
then he became the speed master!
He was as fast as one blink.
He was as green as a pea.
His fangs were as sharp as a knife.
Green Flash was three feet tall,
though he used to be as small as a ball.
Green Flash was scary as a lion.
Green Flash had red fangs at the end of his mouth.
He made people scared,
and made people think it was blood.
He met FireBall at Fire World,
and asked Cool Flash from Land of Monsters,
to rule the world.
FireBall and Cool Flash said, "Yes!"
He also asked Blue Flash,
and he said, "Yes!"

James Agbaje (7)
St Paulinus CE Primary School, Crayford

The School Monster

On a hot, shiny morning
When the friendly monster was flying as high
as a bird
I was walking to school
Ready to learn, when I saw a monster!

When I came into the classroom
My eyes were wide, I saw a monster
An enormous, wild monster
With a scarred face and spikes all over!

"My name is Darkflames," he said
In a quiet voice.
"I came from Crayford because I have nowhere
else."
I felt quite strange, but then I said:
"Okay, you can sit with me and learn well!"

We sat next to each other
He was a generous creature
And I was a genius.
Before we played, we ate together
And happily hopped high.

Luke Pitts (7)
St Paulinus CE Primary School, Crayford

Chicken Stick And The Queen

Chicken Stick was invited to tea by the queen
He flew to the queen's palace
Then dropped from the roof.
"Hello, my highness," said Chicken Stick.
"Greetings, my young friend," replied the queen.

And as Chicken Stick sat down
Like he was on a million pillows
The queen called her royal chef to cook Chicken Stick
Just for the queen to eat Chicken Stick.

And then, at that moment, the queen gobbled him up
Then the queen burped so loud, the whole world shook
So the queen felt silly, smelly, strange and spectacular
Then Chicken Stick jumped out of the queen
And never spoke again.

Zion Makanjuola (8)
St Paulinus CE Primary School, Crayford

The School Monster

On a hot, windy morning
When the tree was laughing
I was walking fast to school
Ready to read and write.
When I came into the classroom
My eyes wide, I saw a smooth and big monster
With flappy wings and fluff.
"My name is Ramflame!" he said
In a fiery voice.
"I came from Raintowiang,
"Because I want to go to school."
I felt quite happy, then I said:
"Okay, you sit with me and learn new things."
We sat next to each other
He then said, "Let's be friends!"
I played with him until we went home.

George Newman (7)
St Paulinus CE Primary School, Crayford

The Age Of Furious Destroyer

On a freaky Friday morning
When the bus was racing to school
I was finally at school
Ready to have a great day at school.

When I came into the classroom
My eyes were wide - I saw a colossal monster!
A monster, it was a scary monster
With an evil grin.

"My name is Furious Destroyer," he said
In a strange voice.
"I came from Populamos
"Because I was being hunted."

"Okay, let's talk."
"But I am hungry..."
"Okay, have some fish!"

Teni Apata (7)
St Paulinus CE Primary School, Crayford

The School Monster

On a wet Friday morning
When the school bus was here
I was on the bus, driving to school
Ready to have a fun day at school.

When I went into the classroom
My eyes were wide open!
I saw an intelligent-looking
Seventeen-eyed monster
With a lot of luggage.

"My name is Harry," he said in an Italian voice.
"I came from home for a lovely day at school."
I felt quite sick, but then I said:
"Okay, you sit with me and feel happy."
We sat next to each other.

William Berry (7)
St Paulinus CE Primary School, Crayford

The Super Hard Wood Monster

My monster is so hard and gross with
a wooden body
He is growing apples all over his body
His eyes are light and also dark
He is so strong that all the sticks can hold him.

His is frightening and really special
He is strange and stinky.
He likes to eat bark and tree trunks
To him, they are like chocolate chip cookies.
He is silly and clever.
He doesn't look perfect and tidy.
He doesn't look soft or smooth or fluffy after all.
He doesn't have horns.
He doesn't fly fast.

Finley Martin (8)
St Paulinus CE Primary School, Crayford

The Tale Of Mr Wizard Blizzard

Once, there was a land called Wizard World,
The trees were very swishy.
In Wizard World, there was a shiny wizard,
He had sharp teeth like a shark,
He was called Mr Wizard Blizzard.

He was as clever as an owl,
He went to school as a happy creature,
The grass was swashy,
He was very good at chopping wood,
He was in a good mood.

The monster queen was coming,
The queen was as beautiful as a flower,
She was as beautiful as a heart,
And she had a crystal-clear crown.

Isaac Rayner (7)
St Paulinus CE Primary School, Crayford

The Monster Who Ran Everywhere

Fast Fred was a large monster
A funny and scary creature
He needed chicken legs to run so fast
All the monsters were jealous of him
But he wasn't jealous of other monsters.

He had smelly breath
He was fast as a cheetah
He had two big eyes like footballs
And he was really greedy
He was really brave too.

When he went to France, driving a car
The people were really scared
But he said he was a friendly monster
And they all went away with smiles on their faces.

Ben Butler (8)
St Paulinus CE Primary School, Crayford

How Monsters Are Born

A spotty egg cracked open one day in a hurry
Just like bric-a-brak
They had to take care of it before it boiled
They rumbled, tumbled and crumbled.

She grew up like a lion
She was intelligent at monster school
She was cute and brave
But always got back late.

People called her a gentle, friendy and soft cat
Her mum and dad called her a skinny,
jolly creature
Even though she didn't like it
Her enemies called her a ragged, huge and
silly creature.

Olivia Makanjuola (8)
St Paulinus CE Primary School, Crayford

The School Monster

On a hot morning
When the kind monster was running
I was running really fast to school
Ready to get in the classroom.

When I came into the classroom
My eyes were wide
I saw an enormous monster
A gigantic monster!
I was with my best friend.

"My name is Dead Killer," he said
In an angry voice.
"I came from Spain because I like this school."
I felt quite scared, but then I said:
"Okay, you sit with me and read a story."

Ronnie Bruce (8)
St Paulinus CE Primary School, Crayford

If Only A Monster

If you want to be a fluffy monster
you need to be so brave and strong
and make the other monsters happy.

If you want to be a fluffy monster
you have to live in the forest
and be fluffy and cute.

If you want to be a fluffy monster
you have to be clever
and be skinny.

Fluffy is a naughty monster
with sharp teeth.

He likes to dig holes and can be cheeky sometimes
he goes outside to dig holes.

Bracken Rutter (8)
St Paulinus CE Primary School, Crayford

Merairy And The Monster Pixie

Once, there was a beautiful monster, Merairy
Who loved to swim and fly
She loved to swim with mermaids
And fly in the sky.

She was clever as an owl
Who loved to hang on the trees in the sky.

Once, there were monster pixies
Who had wings to fly across the sky.

One day, Merairy flew across the sky
To visit the Monster Pixie Village
She saw a monster pixie trying to fly
So she went to see who it was...

Delina Yosief (8)
St Paulinus CE Primary School, Crayford

The Destructible Man In Sight

My monster's name is Jacky
Watch him, he is scrappy
With seven legs! He is hacky
He is Jacky.

On a Saturday morning
He met someone scrappy
And very happy.

He didn't have a friend
But he just made one
He was as thin as tin
He was as quiet as a mouse.

They were arguing about a token
With a Chinese star on it.
The star had shiny shoes
And Jacky got it.

Emmanuel Sanusi (7)
St Paulinus CE Primary School, Crayford

The Treasure Hunt

One day, walking back from school
I saw a monster
He smelt like volcano rocks
He was called Mr Happy and he was a
little bit smiley
He liked apple pies and he wore ties.

We went to the park
The park was as big as two houses
Mr Happy saw a clue on the swing
It had an arrow pointing to the left which was red.

We found another clue
It was as long as a snake
Mr Happy read it, it said:
'Treasure under the pile of rocks.'
One rock was shiny, so Mr Happy lifted up the rock
And under the rock was a treasure chest
There was a map
And it led to a key
It said to go to space.

On our way to space, we saw the key
We took it, then we went back to the park
And we opened the chest and there were
bars of gold
And we built a house with them.

Mollie Moore (8)

St Simon's RC Primary School, South Ashford

The Lost Home

Once, there lived an alien,
He had three eyes,
He was a baby,
And he was wearing ties.

The monster was as light as a feather,
And he sat on leather.

There was an earthquake,
The ground shrivelled up like a raisin,
His mother died, so he was going to Earth,
With his friends Ling and Bing.

They got to Earth,
Where they found a deep, dark hole,
That was home to a mole,
They made friends,
And lived there forever!

Lorena Francesca Bulla (8)
St Simon's RC Primary School, South Ashford

Miggy Fuzz Lee's Time Out Play

Sleeping slow and lying in bed
I was dreaming of strawberries red
Until I heard a stomp as loud as a whale
It was raining and pouring with hail.

Suddenly, I woke up with a scream
The weird monster gave me ice cream
It had four eyes and a big mouth
He said, "I live in the south."

His name was Miggy Fuzz Lee
Then I heard a buzz as loud as a bee
We went outside and had some fun
Then we went out and chewed bubblegum.

Zhyanne Sevilla (8)
St Simon's RC Primary School, South Ashford

The Adventure To Earth

One day, I saw a rocket,
It landed with a boom.
I asked where he was from,
He said, "Moon."
Then he squeaked, "I flew away from Blob!"
I said, "You look like a mop."
The monster said, "I know."
He asked to stay at my home.
I said, "Of course!"
I gave him lunch
With a little pouch.
He said, "Blob left slime
In a line,
On the road,
Where there was a toad."

Karolina Grudzien (8)
St Simon's RC Primary School, South Ashford

The Monster

He lives on the moon
And his name is Slimy Samy
Every year he eats humans.

His friend is next door
He has no other friends
Slimy Samy went to Earth.

He got an ice cream
Slimy Samy found a child
And ate him all up
He slept like a lion.

He never woke up
He stayed like a log
Forever, the people weren't afraid any more.

Evie Miller (7)
St Simon's RC Primary School, South Ashford

The Little Mission

My little monster is called Mr Little
He is as small as a kitten
My monster has no friends

Mr Little lives in a big house
It is as big as a hotel
Mr Little is good, but no one knows

Mr Little wants to say
That he is good as a sunny day
No one listened to him
So he just went and had a play.

Anna Repinska (8)
St Simon's RC Primary School, South Ashford

The Misunderstood

I met a monster, then I heard people say:
"He is as red as blood."
"He is as smelly as a dog."
"He is as loud as a bear."

Teeth as sharp as knives
A grin as cheeky as your little brother
Horns as grey as rocks
Wings as dark as the cave
Eyes as blue as the sea.

Madison Moore (8)
St Simon's RC Primary School, South Ashford

Monster

M y monster is slimy
O n dark, snowy nights my monster creepts
N o one can stop my monster
S ometimes my monster kills
T he monster is scary
E very day my monster eats people
R ed-eyed monster.

Dawid Szarafinski (8)
St Simon's RC Primary School, South Ashford

The Gooey Volcano

The Gooey Volcano
was born in a mouldy volcano.

A green, slimy monster
with goo coming out of his skin.

Black, red and grey
and goes out in windy, rainy nights.

Alicia Pawlowska Louis (8)
St Simon's RC Primary School, South Ashford

Looks Do Not Matter!

Kaikaya lived in a deep, dark cave
She was really nice and loved to play
But the only trouble was
Kaikaya had no one to play with every day
For the stupid humans
Didn't like the look of her
As she was a monster.
Looks do not matter; I'm really nice
Kaikaya thought
Will they ever learn?

Then, one day, Kaikaya thought
While eating her breakfast (cornflakes with honey)
I'll leave my cave and show humans I'm harmless
And that I don't wreck things and don't cost them
money.
So off she went
First stop, Paris
She drove there
In a red Toyota Yaris.

As she drove, she was full of joy
Then as she arrived in Paris, France
She was very happy
She wanted to dance!
As she got out of her car
People told her she was cute
And very different
And from the Eiffel Tower, people waved.

She was interviewed in New York City
On Good Morning America
While stroking her new kitty
Which she'd bought in Paris.
She was asked a question by Lily Nooks
Kaikara said
"Well, Lily, looks
Do not matter!"

Louise Hobbs (10)
The Academy Of Woodlands, Gillingham

Tim Is My Friend

The dragon had five eyes and was naughty,
He was my friend, but he was ever so stinky,
This dragon's name was Tim,
His face was always so grim,
But whatever the weather, I could always make
him smile,
And that made me feel good inside for a while.

Its skin was red like the blazing sun,
Tim's talons were sharp and never blunt.
Tim was not bad inside - he was soft,
But don't get on his bad side, or he'd give
you a shock!

He had a big mouth and forked tongue,
Don't talk back, or you'd get a thump.

Tim was my friend and a great one, too.
I loved him like a cow loves to moo!

Samuel Adewumi-Abogunloko (10)
The Academy Of Woodlands, Gillingham

When I Go To Bed

When I go to bed
I feel a clawing at my toes
my cheeks puff air and my nose goes bright red
I feel really, really scared
and I think my mum knows
that monsters come out when light switches
are closed.

I see red eyes that glint in the dark
I don't know how many - one, two or three
but I know that they're there, 'cause they leave a
nasty mark
but as I look closer, I see that they vary.
One is green, one is blue and once I even saw one
with the flu!

I've learnt to live with these nasty beasts
after all, they only get the feet!

Rhea Gowda (10)
The Academy Of Woodlands, Gillingham

The Day Of Bad And Good Monsters

It was as cold as Antarctica with snow
The good and the bad monsters were rivals
In the morning glow
Flonty had left home to help the bad monsters.

Before he found the crew, he saw a baby
It was a good one
He left the crew behind maybe
He was as good as dead.

Flonty said to him, "Hello?"
There was no answer and he was changing
Into a good monster. The baby replied, "Hello?"
It was now a yeti!

Flonty's long tongue carried them home
To a cave
The yeti then changed again
Into Flonty's gnome.

Anton Williams (10)
The Academy Of Woodlands, Gillingham

The Little Monster

A little egg rolled in a net,
Crack! The egg fell and a foot came out.
Crack! again, out came the rest.
There was the fluffy monster,
Ready to go.
Bump! She landed at someone's feet.

She ended up in a little cage,
The shadow took her in her hands,
Then she got told, "Behave!"
Was she a pet?

Little Doki ran away,
Hoping she could stay awake,
Her fox tail now grew out,
She looked at the Monster Village,
"This is what my life's about."

Grace Waters (9)
The Academy Of Woodlands, Gillingham

Fluff The Fluffy, Flying Cloud

I am Fluff,
I live somewhere blue,
not in the sea
but in the sky.
When I'm sad,
you all see.
When I'm angry,
I shock you so bad,
that you wee.
When I'm happy,
I treat you to a free tan.

Night and day come so quickly,
but when I'm up to mischief,
anything is possible.
Every now and then,
you might hear people say,
"It's five o'clock!
Why isn't it dark?"

And while my time passes,
I think to myself,
Why do I bother?
and my brother chuckles.

Ini Caoimhe Rowaiye (10)
The Academy Of Woodlands, Gillingham

The Fluff Monster

Very young
Just eight months old
He stands out from others
He is very bold

He's a good monster
Not bad at all
Not like his parents
Because they are tall

He comes from a lagoon
That's why he's blue
If it's your birthday
He'll give presents to you

He has bright pink cheeks
With fluffy orange hair
He is kind and warm
With love to share

He hasn't many friends
Because most monsters are bad
Which makes him think
Are they mad?

Victoria Streater (9)
The Academy Of Woodlands, Gillingham

The World Is Not All Happiness

Meet Rainbow, she's a monster
well, don't be scared, she's a good guy
her favourite food is lobster
and she really wishes to fly.

Well, she was kicked out of adoption about three
months ago
so she let her life flow
with joy and happiness
but her flying dream didn't die.

One day, she decided she'd fly
like that bird in the sky.
She did it!
But then she said, "I don't want to die!"
And she lay there and saw
the world was not all cupcakes and rainbows.

Ashton Boothroyd (9)
The Academy Of Woodlands, Gillingham

Lazerbeam

There was once a huge monster,
Who was on every wanted poster,
He was very clever,
But he thought he was as light as a feather.
He would shape-shift,
Then he would lift,
Little children into the air,
And they would scream, "It's not fair!"
He would *chomp, chomp, chomp,*
And they would bonk,
Him on the head,
While he said,
"Why is this happening to me?"
So, you see,
Whilst you have a cup of tea,
Lazerbeam is bad,
Like what he never had.

Lily Dance (10)
The Academy Of Woodlands, Gillingham

The Depressed Icaron

The beast was massive!
You may have had a fright
And if it wasn't positive
It could put up a good fight!

Its head was as big as a whale
With its body tripled
The tail had spikes and scales
With legs quadruple.

One day, it got bored
So it went to Paris
And it explored
It met a person called Harris.

Then, on a miserable day
Mr Harris was declared dead
His only ever friend, Icaron, was in a bad way
His friend's grave he gifted a piece of bread.

Kyle Rabey Sumpter (9)
The Academy Of Woodlands, Gillingham

The Cookie Cream Adventure

There once was a monster called Cookie Cream,
It was round, brown and never mean.
I should know, because I saw it gleam,
In the jungle of the good King Cream.

It had cute eyes that shone,
A round body with legs and arms,
It was fluffy - or should I say, very fluffy,
It was the cutest thing on Earth.

Its friends were just as cute,
Although, they made me want to press mute.
They were so loud, one wore a boot!
Did I mention that they were cute?

Grace Mackenney (10)
The Academy Of Woodlands, Gillingham

The Best Friend I Ever Had

Don't be afraid of monsters,
Not all are bad,
I have one as a friend,
The best friend I ever had.

His name is Googly,
He is as fluffy as can be,
Googly has three googly eyes,
Comes with the name, as you can see.

Sometimes he can be naughty,
He jumps up on my bed,
People think he is cute,
Even though he sits on my head!

Don't be afraid of monsters,
Not all are bad!
I have Googly,
The best friend I ever had!

Taylor-Marie Daws (10)
The Academy Of Woodlands, Gillingham

My Moo Moo

Don't worry, she's not bad
But she can be a bit mad
Out in the backyard
Playing with her favourite colourful cards

Never eating her peas
But always playing with the bees
Just maybe bumping into a few trees

It's the loving llama
Who brought joy
To the amazing world of toys

Once, Moo Moo was sad
But the loving llama laughed
A smile filled Moo Moo's face
It was just a small pace.

Jaslyn Kaur Parmar (10)
The Academy Of Woodlands, Gillingham

Lunchtime With Broot

My monster is tall and green,
He is extremely mean.
Munch! Munch! Munch!
Crunch! Crunch! Crunch!
Don't leave food outside
When it's nearly lunch.

He is as tall as a full-grown sunflower,
Guess what? He never has a shower!
Broot plays the flute;
Whenever he plays
It makes the owls hoot.

He has big eyes
And has a snout like a horse's.
The head of him is like a saucer.

Bobbie Robertson-Stanley (10)
The Academy Of Woodlands, Gillingham

The New Things

Lenny is his name,
he doesn't have any fame,
his cave is cold as ice,
he comes out one night,
to see there's more than mice,
there are friends and foes,
with more than three toes,
evil and good,
there's wood,
and trees,
and tiny peas,
holly and the beautiful bees,
there are cities which are busy,
and there are maps and caps,
there are cars that they mend,
and beginnings and ends.

Josh S Kirby (9)
The Academy Of Woodlands, Gillingham

The Lonely Monster

A little orange monster was born in a bush
He was so clever and fluffy
So he kicked and pushed
Then he was rolling out.

He looked around for someone to play
A little kid pushed him over
Then fell in a pile of hay
The hay got taken to a farm with him in there.

At the farm, he got so scared
It was a stormy night
He had a nightmare
While sleeping, the storm stopped.

Lexi Lowin (9)
The Academy Of Woodlands, Gillingham

Scary Monster! Stay Back!

As you stroll through the wood,
His four eyes glow,
Like four torches,
Staring right at you.

His three feet run,
As fast as you can imagine,
Chasing after you,
Like you're having fun.

Stay back,
Otherwise, get eaten,
I'm just warning you,
It's up to you.

He lives in the bottom of a volcano,
That's why he's so hot.

Holly Watson (10)
The Academy Of Woodlands, Gillingham

Big Mouth's Personality

Big Mouth never has a frown
Don't give him a bill which is foul
His favourite thing to do is hang upside down
If he gets dizzy, he will have a little growl

If you feed him beans
He will get the flu
If his body turns bright green
His face will turn dark blue

Don't backchat
He will get angry
Or a little fat
Maybe a bit fancy.

Chloe Higgins (9)
The Academy Of Woodlands, Gillingham

Freaky Green

Slimy creature made from slime
He's so good, he's never done a crime
He's dumb as a sponge
Don't worry, he's fine

He has no friends
He's not mean
No one wants to be his friend
'Cause he's green

He's really nice
He's green and fluffy
But he's got head lice.

Jago Herd (10)
The Academy Of Woodlands, Gillingham

My Monster

My monster is quite small
Some say he's quite tall
Some say he's got fiery eyes from his dad
But some say he's only sad.

My monster wears green shorts
And flies from the monster port
My monster says he's cool
And some say he's a fool.

George Collins (10)
The Academy Of Woodlands, Gillingham

Mumble Jumble And Blurgorb's Trash

The Blorgorb is here!
I don't exactly know if he has ears.
Yes, he is scary!
Oh, and stupidly hairy!
Not to mention, he is lazy and crazy
He came from an asylum
So he has some rare items.

Lots of people shout, "Look at him!"
Just because he can't swim
He's very nimble
He's a pretty monster
But he's still single.

Once, he tried to eat my cats
My rugs
My mats
He, however, doesn't eat rats!
(No animals are harmed.)

Brady Aaron Chapman (9)
Tree Tops Academy, Park Wood

My Monster Called Jeff

My monster is furry, he comes from Jupiter,
He's good at basketball
He has super powers called 'Criss cross apple sauce'
(You have to say it in an American accent for it to rhyme)
He doesn't just speak English
He also speaks Jupitallio
My monster is full of fur
(Only on half of his body)
He's half a cat and can purr
He's also good at hockey
He loves school and has a teacher called Mrs Lockey
My monster's name is
Jeffy.

Kieran Aaron Byrne (10)
Tree Tops Academy, Park Wood

Mischievous Maggie

I met a mischievous monster,
She had six beady eyes,
And she was sure that,
Monsters would soon arise.
She befriended a snail,
It rode on her tail,
They went to the park,
When it was late at night and dark.
She had a trick up her sleeve,
One you won't believe,
She killed the snail,
With her sharp tail.
She didn't feel bad at all,
She took a picture and,
Put it on the wall.

Tayla Champion (10)
Tree Tops Academy, Park Wood

Draco

I am Draco
I go to the park
Where there are larks
Not any sharks

I can breathe fire
As it's my desire
I go to the pool
Because I am cool

I can be a fool
If I use tools
I like pools
And building stools

I like lime
Plus some slime
I like Nike
And my bike

I have a plan
That I've made with Sam

To take over the world
Using a cord we've curled.

Amon Rai (9)
Tree Tops Academy, Park Wood

A Monster Called Cuddles

A monster called Cuddles,
loves splashing in puddles,
and loves big cuddles.
I met her in Spain,
but she was standing in the rain.
I took her to school,
then we went to the pool.
I took her home,
but my mum moaned,
then we went to the park,
but it was dark,
then Cuddles had to go.
I hope I see her again,
at least, she said I will.

Chelsea Mount (10)
Tree Tops Academy, Park Wood

Fuzz

A monster called Fuzz
as tall as a tree
came down from space
to see me
he never gives up
as brave as a lion.

He's from space
what do I say?
He's fuzzy and lovely
but if you give him a tart
he would rather fart.

Fuzz is my friend
he never gives up
he counts on me
that's why we call him Fuzz.

Emma-Louise Matthews (10)
Tree Tops Academy, Park Wood

When Gorger Came To School

When Gorger came to school,
He broke every rule,
He was a big green monster,
Two feet tall,
He ate all the plungers,
Broke all the stools,
He hated all the teachers,
Messed up all the floors,
Then along came Mrs Manvile,
Then Mrs Norman to save the day,
Flattened him right out,
Then he ran away!

Maddison Scott (10)
Tree Tops Academy, Park Wood

Bongo

I met Bongo
on the way to school
he was so ugly
but he was very cool
he was so slimy
I said, "Oh, blimey!"

I was in class
so was he
he said to Miss
"I need a wee wee."

When he came back
he was so tall
he was the tallest
in our school.

Toby-Lee William Prebble (9)
Tree Tops Academy, Park Wood

My Friend Is A Monster

He smiles like Prince Charles
calls goodnight, but bites
comes from another dimension
eats foundation
loves my mum's Sensations.

Yes, he is ugly
doesn't mean he isn't funny.

My friend goes to school
hits the hall
even though he's really tall.

William Steel (10)
Tree Tops Academy, Park Wood

My Fire Monster Sparks

I have a fire-breathing monster
His name is Sparks
He is born in lava
He can't die, except in cold places
He hates sparklers

Sparks spits fire
He sits on fire
He has the power to teleport
We got to school and he burnt everything
He is cooler than Donald Trump.

Taohil Islam (9)
Tree Tops Academy, Park Wood

Fluff-Puff

When I brought Fluff-Puff to school
everyone thought I was a fool.
But when my monster came through the door
the teacher dropped dead on the floor.
I didn't get it, she was cute and pink
but when she came through the door
nobody dared to blink.

Dibya Rai (10)
Tree Tops Academy, Park Wood

The Prince's Baby

When I was sitting on my chair
I heard a noise from under there
It sounded like a bear
I looked under the table
She had purple and pink eyes
And blue, fluffy, soft fur
With a red hat and flowers.

Faith Edmonds (10)
Tree Tops Academy, Park Wood

Cutie Pie

I saw a magical monster,
She lives on Planet Fluffy,
She is very pretty,
She is cute just like a kitty,
When she eats her lunch her teeth get really sharp,
She likes listening to the wonderful harp.

Kayley Watt (10)
Tree Tops Academy, Park Wood

On My Way To School

I am on my way to school
I hear a big boom
it is a monster, the name
is Jeffrey. He has six eyes
that are red and he is kind
to people, it has a demon tail
has claws and demon wings.

Joshua Baldock (9)
Tree Tops Academy, Park Wood

The Hungry Monster

There is a monster that lives under my bed
She gets very hangry if she is not fed
She doesn't like to be disturbed
I can't even say a word

I have to feed her once a day
Or she will come out to play
She is quite nice
She likes chasing lots of mice

I like playing with her
But if I called her 'sir'
She would probably bite my head off!
At least I would not have a cough!

I must tell you something
You see
The monster is actually me!

Amelia Joyce Mitchell (10)
Wickham Court School, West Wickham